THE ULTIMATE SPY CLUB™

The Stakeout
Spying & Secret Surveillance

by Red Cordello

with Tony and Jonna Mendez
Consultants

Scholastic Inc.
New York • Toronto • London • Auckland • Sydney
Mexico City • New Delhi • Hong Kong • Buenos Aires

ISBN 0-439-90851-5

Designer: Aruna Goldstein
Illustrations: James W. Elston
Comic Strip Illustrations: Yancey Labat

Photos: Page 9: Reuters/Corbis. Page 22: Bettman/Corbis.
Page 23: Bettman/Corbis. Page 30: International Spy Museum.

12 11 10 9 8 7 6 5 4 3 2 1 7 8 9 10 11/0

Printed in the U.S.A.

First printing, March 2007

The publisher has made every effort to ensure that the activities in this book are safe when done as instructed. Children are encouraged to do their spy activities with willing friends and family members and to respect others' right to privacy. Adults should provide guidance and supervision whenever the activity requires.

Table of Contents

A Spy's Eyes

Need to figure out what that secret is your brother's hiding? Want to find out what Mom is getting you for your birthday? Well, have no fear. Real spies use all sorts of tricks to watch their targets and get the info they need, from hiding in trees to using electronic listening devices. They have special techniques for following someone without being noticed and to make sure they're not being followed. And they use gadgets like disguises, binoculars, and even **bugs**!

You've learned a lot through your spy training, but now it's time to go out into the field. With your latest **Ultimate Spy Club** handbook and spy kit, you'll learn about...

Tailing

Sometimes spies need to watch someone as they move around to see where they're going and who they meet up with. You'll learn a special technique to follow and observe a moving target that involves a **rabbit**, a tail, a point, and a wing.

Setting Up Surveillance

You'll learn how to set up a special spot where you can sit comfortably while getting the important info you need!

Surveillance Detection

It's important to make sure no one is watching you or your HQ! Good spies know lots of **surveillance** and **countersurveillance** tricks, so it's nearly impossible to spy on them while they spy on others.

And more!

Be sure to visit the **Ultimate Spy Club** online at:
www.scholastic.com/ultimatespy

This month's secret password is:
eyesandears

What's in Your *Spy Kit?*

Your spy kit contains two Ultimate Spy Club gadgets:

Spy Ear

This special listening device will let you hear what's being said from far away. You won't miss any important info, and no one will be the wiser.

Folding Binoculars

These binoculars can help you see important things while letting you keep your distance. And when you're not using them, you can fold them up and slip them into your pocket. No one will suspect a thing, and you'll always be ready to run surveillance!

MISSION #1: LOOK AND LISTEN

Real spies use surveillance to follow enemy spies and get important information. They have to see what the enemy's up to while keeping them in the dark. Spies can set up a safe place to watch from, follow the enemy, or plant special devices to let them sit back and observe.

A good spy not only knows how to watch without being seen, but also what things to pay attention to. It's very important to notice anything out of place. Lots of normal-looking activities could turn out to be important. A person tying their shoe could be a signal, and that piece of paper that was just thrown in the trash could be a note to another spy.

With the spy tricks you'll learn, you'll be an expert at surveillance and be able to get all the info and evidence you need.

Surveillance 101

There are all kinds of surveillance out there, which means it's important to pick the right type for your situation. Once you've figured out who your surveillance **target** is and where you'll be trying to watch them, take a look and come up with a top-notch surveillance plan.

Static Surveillance: Staying Put

Static surveillance is when you stay in one spot, watching one spot. You can use this to watch another spy's HQ to see who goes in and out of it, or to watch an area where strange things are happening. When you conduct static surveillance, it's best to set up a **surveillance post**—a place where you and your fellow spies can sit comfortably and watch without being noticed.

Mobile Surveillance: For the Spy on the Go!

Mobile surveillance is when you're following a moving target, like another spy, to find something out (like where his HQ is or who he's meeting). Sometimes you'll need the help of other spies to make sure you're not caught during your surveillance operation.

Audiovisual

You have to use all of your senses and observation skills when conducting surveillance, but your eyes and ears are the most important. Visual surveillance can involve taking photos, or even using periscopes or telescopes. Anything that watches, from security cameras in a bank to your Great Aunt Edna keeping an eye on her cats, is visual surveillance.

Audio surveillance is all about getting information you hear. Audio surveillance can be anything from listening to people talk around you to using hidden microphones and tape recorders.

Real Spy Gadgets

Talk about spying from a distance! Today, spies can use satellites in outer space to conduct visual surveillance. This picture was taken by a satellite over Washington, DC. Can you spot the Washington Monument?

Set Up a Spy Post!

Need to keep an eye on a certain spot for a while? Then it's time to set up a surveillance post and start doing some static surveillance. A surveillance post is a place where you can watch your target for long periods of time without being seen. It can be someplace simple, like a tree house, or someplace harder to hide, like behind a bush.

Setting the Spot

When choosing where to set up your spy post, you need to make sure you've got a good view of the spot you're watching and that your surveillance post will keep you hidden from view. It's important to make sure you're comfortable, because you'll be there making your observations for a while. You also want

to make sure you can get in and out of your spy post without being spotted, in case you need to get home or take a break.

Test it Out

Make sure no one can see you in your spy post by having a friend walk by while you're inside. If they can see you, try to sit differently so you aren't seen. Or try changing your clothes so you'll blend into your surroundings. If you're in a tree, you can wear green and maybe even tape some leaves and branches to your clothes and hat.

SPY TIP:

Remember, it's always important to respect other people's privacy. Some people won't want you listening in or taking their photo. Always ask for permission before practicing your surveillance skills.

Come Equipped!

Bring all the spy gear you'll need and a notebook to jot down what you see and hear. Make notes of everything that happens. If you're staking out an enemy spy's HQ, write down who goes in and out, and what they're holding and wearing. If you get tired or hungry, try taking turns with a co-spy. Or, if your spy post is big enough, you can both spy from it together!

SPY HISTORY UNCOVERED

When the FBI needed to run surveillance on suspected **mole** Robert Hannsen, they found the perfect spy post for their static surveillance. They moved into the house across the street!

Follow the Rabbit!

Get some friends and practice this key technique for mobile surveillance and following your target. You're going to be the ABC Team, because you'll be doing **ABC surveillance**. ABC surveillance involves four people—your target (the person you'll be following), and a three-person surveillance team, each in a different position. Each position involved has a special name:

- **The Rabbit.** The Rabbit is your target, or the person you'll be following.

- **The Point.** The Point is the person who walks closest behind the Rabbit.

- **The Tail.** The Tail follows behind the Point and will take his place if necessary.

- **The Wing.** The wing follows the Rabbit and the rest of the surveillance team from across the street to make sure everything's going okay. They're always ready to jump in if they need to.

With all these people and this special technique, the Rabbit never has to find out they're being followed!

Before you start following, you'll need to decide which position each of you will take (don't worry, you'll probably be rotating them once you start). It's also important to decide on a few special signals before you get started.

Make sure that you're using this technique on foot (it would look silly on roller skates) and in a relatively crowded area. Otherwise, the Rabbit will be able to see all of you easily. Also, make sure a senior spy (an adult) knows where you're going in case they need to send reinforcements!

Tail 'Em

Now, start following the Rabbit. Make sure the Point always has the Rabbit in sight, but doesn't look too suspicious. The Tail (behind the Point) doesn't need to have the Rabbit in her sights. If at any time the Point thinks that the Rabbit has spotted him, it's time to rotate! The Point should give the Tail a signal, like bending down to tie his shoelace. Then, the Tail should walk past the Point and become the *new* Point, following behind the Rabbit. The old Point is now the Tail. This way, the Rabbit won't ever see the same person following them!

If the Rabbit goes into a store, or stops to tie his shoelace, he might be testing to see if you're following him. The Point should make a hand signal and let the Tail know that the Rabbit has stopped. Then, the Point should keep walking past the Rabbit. If the Point stops, the Rabbit will know something weird is going on! Then the Tail can walk slowly until the Rabbit starts moving again. The Tail becomes the Point, and the old Point can duck around a corner (and maybe even change into a simple disguise) and wait for the Point to pass him. Then, he can step back out and become the new Tail.

If at any time, the Tail loses sight of the Point, or the Point loses sight of the Rabbit, then the Wing should swoop in and take over. Make sure the Wing knows it's okay to do this with a hand signal.

With practice, you should be able to use ABC surveillance to follow anyone. It'll be as easy as, well, ABC!

SPY TIP:

Here are some good signals you can use when conducting ABC surveillance. They look natural, and can be seen from far away.

- **Stop to tie your shoelace**
- **Remove a jacket or sweatshirt**
- **Put on a hat**
- **Stretch your arms over your head**
- **Drop something and stop to pick it up**

Don't forget to decide on what each signal means and make sure everybody in your group knows before you get started! What other signals can you think of?

Eye Spy

There are many different tools to assist spies in visual surveillance—telescopes, binoculars, periscopes, and of course, cameras. The problem with cameras is that you can usually tell when someone is taking a picture with one—not a very good thing if you're trying to spy! Because of this, spies use a lot of different tools and tricks like hidden cameras and special shooting techniques to make it look like they're not taking pictures (or at least not pictures of anything important!).

Top Secret Tourists

Sometimes, spies will dress up like tourists and make it look like they're taking pictures of their friends or tourist sites. Really, they're just pointing the camera at their friends—they're *focusing* the camera on important things behind them. Try it with some friends: have them pose for you and make it look like you're taking photos of them. Then really take pictures of the things behind them.

Be a Hip Photographer

Sometimes, when it isn't safe to even look like they're taking photos, spies use a trick called **shooting from the hip**.

This is when you don't bring the camera to your eye, but hold it at your hip, and take photos without looking. This sort of photography takes a lot of practice (and don't forget to make sure the flash is off!). With time, you should be able to take photos without making it look like you're using your camera at all.

Candid Camera

There are times when even holding a camera can be suspicious, so spies have to come up with ways to hide it completely. Here are great ways to take some secret photos.

- With an adult's permission, cut a small hole in the pocket of an old jacket. Place the camera in the pocket and try taking photos through the hole. It will just look like you have your hands in your pockets!

You can also try hiding your camera in a lunch bag or a bag of snacks with a small hole cut in it. (Ask and adult first!) Empty out the bag, put the camera in, and then put the snacks back on top. When you reach in for some food, snap the photo. Then take out some food and eat it—no one will think you're doing anything but snacking!

A small hole torn in a magazine or newspaper can also let you observe and take photos without being noticed.

SPY TIP:

Try practicing taking photos from all sorts of angles without looking through the camera—around corners and even over walls. You can also pair your camera with a mirror or a periscope. What does your camera see that you can't?

Scope it Out!

Cameras aren't the only tools spies use for visual surveillance. With the aid of a periscope, spies can see around corners and over walls. You can make a periscope using two old milk cartons, two small mirrors, and some tape. Get an adult to help you out with this one.

You Need:

- ✔ 2 rinsed-out milk cartons
- ✔ Scissors
- ✔ Tape
- ✔ 2 small mirrors (these can be found in most drug stores)

⇨ Have an adult help you cut off the top of each carton.

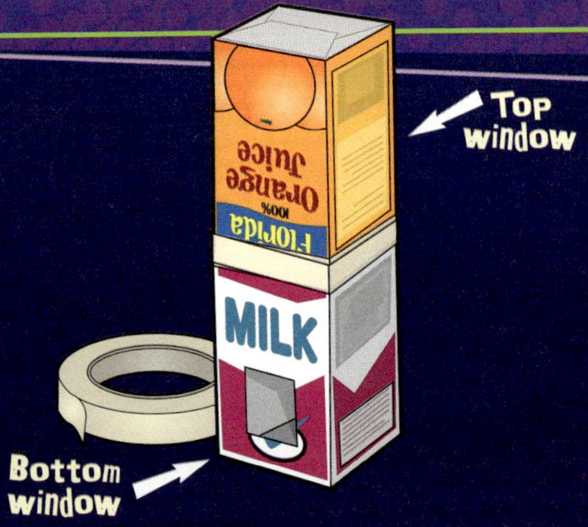

⇨ Tape the open parts of the two cartons together. This should leave you with one long rectangular box.

⇨ Next you need to cut two windows in the box for you to look through. Have an adult help you cut out one window on the front at the bottom, and one on the back at the top.

⇨ Now take the two mirrors and hold them beside the box at the level of the two windows. With the reflective sides facing one another and your eye at the level of the bottom window, adjust the mirrors until you can see into the top mirror by looking into the bottom mirror. Mark the angles of the mirrors on the side of the periscope.

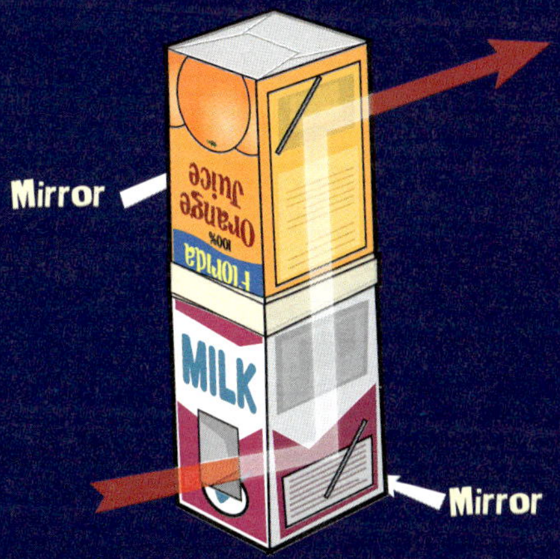

Now cut a slit in each side of the box along this line and slide the mirrors into place. Look through the bottom window of the periscope. You should be able to see out the top window using the two mirrors. If not, try adjusting the mirrors some more.

When it's working, tape the mirrors into place.

With some practice, you should be able to look into one end and see out the other. You can use this periscope to see around corners or over walls! Now try taking a photo through the periscope. How did it come out?

Listening In

If you've ever heard what your friends were whispering or tried to listen in on a conversation, that's audio surveillance. Audio surveillance can be just as useful as visual surveillance. With electronic bugs (listening devices), spies can listen to enemy plans as if they're right at the table with them!

When you're conducting surveillance, whether it's visual or mobile, at some point your target will stop and talk with someone. You want to listen, of course, but if you get too close, you'll blow your cover. This is where your Spy Ear comes in handy. The Spy Ear picks up audio vibrations and then amplifies them—sort of like what happens when you talk into a paper cone. Here are some clever ways to make sure you don't miss a word!

⇨ Try putting your ear next to a heating vent. Can you hear people on a different floor of your house? Try pairing this up with your Spy Ear. Does that make things louder?

SPY HISTORY UNCOVERED

In China, people used to make special chimneys that would let them hear things in the other room, sort of like how heating vents can be used today.

If you need to hear what's going on in another room, try putting your Spy Ear by the opening at the bottom of a closed door.

You can use a glass to help you hear through walls. First, put the open end of a glass up against the wall.

Then, put your ear to the bottom of the glass. This works like your Spy Ear by amplifying the vibrations voices make against the wall.

Real Spy Gadgets

Some spies have special pinhole drills that let them plant tiny microphones in the walls of the people next door. Some super high tech spies use invisible lasers, which they bounce off their enemy's windows. The windows vibrate when people talk, and that makes the laser vibrate. Then, the spies can translate the laser vibrations back into words from a long way away.

SPY HISTORY UNCOVERED

The Berlin Tunnel: Operation Gold

Sometimes, the simplest plans are the best. Digging a giant tunnel into enemy territory to listen to what's going on above might sound like a silly idea, but for a little while, it worked!

During the Cold War, the CIA and British Intelligence worked together to dig a tunnel 1,476 feet long, under the wall that divided East and West Germany. There, they used electronic surveillance to listen in on secret Soviet intelligence for an entire year. They overheard their phone calls and coded messages and sent them back to Washington DC to try to figure them out. They recorded half a million

phone calls on 50,000 tapes. For a little while, it worked great. But then, the Germans found the tunnel!

The Germans, were pretty clever, too. Instead of just showing the Americans they had found the secret tunnel, they decided to use it to pass along **misinformation**—fake codes and messages. The American spies spent a long time trying to decode these messages, only to find out that the information they thought they had was wrong!

A year after the tunnel went into use, the Germans decided to reveal it to the entire world, forcing the American spies to retreat. The Americans may have had a clever idea, but the Germans knew how to turn the tables.

Subtle Spying

Your Spy Ear might attract some attention if you're out in public. That's why it's important to learn how to use it as subtly as possible.

A Disguise

Since it already has earphones, why not disguise your Spy Ear as an MP3 player? You can hide it in an MP3 player case if you have one, or you can make one out of construction paper and cardboard. Then you can pretend to be looking at your MP3 player while you position it and listen in. No one will suspect you of listening to anything but your favorite music!

Spy Ear Extras

Here are some other important tips to help keep your spying under wraps.

- You have to point your Spy Ear in the direction of what you're listening to for it to work best. If your Spy Ear stays clipped at your waist, you can change your own position rather than having to move it around with your hand.
- If you need to have the Spy Ear in your hand, try to hold it so the sound dish faces out while your hand keeps the rest of the listening device covered up.

MISSION #2: TURNING THE TABLE

Now you know how to follow and watch your enemies—but be careful! They know how to watch you, too. What if someone's running surveillance on you? What if *you're* the Rabbit?

How can you make sure no one's out to get your secrets? And how can you be sure no one's listening in on your important conversations? Real spies use a ton of tricks to make sure no one is listening to or watching them.

Learn these techniques and with a little practice, you'll be able to defeat even a master spy's surveillance tricks.

A Counter-Spy Experiment

It's very important for a spy to make sure they aren't being watched. While they're out looking for info on their targets, other spies are often looking for info on them. That's why spies have developed all sorts of techniques to help them know if they're being watched.

Throw Them Off

The main way to tell if you're being followed is by using a **Surveillance Detection Run** or **SDR**. This is when you go outside and walk around to find out if someone is watching you. You can use reflective surfaces like mirrors and store

Pop Culture

In the film *The Lady from Shanghai*, the title character, knowing she is being followed, goes into a house of mirrors to throw off the man who is following her.

or stop into a store to buy a pack of gum in order to check for spies. When you stop, it will force anyone following you to make a decision. They'll either have to walk on by or stop. If you choose to stop into a store, you'll have a chance to look around freely before continuing on your way.

windows to help you look behind you. If you carry a mirror with you, you can pull it out and pretend to be looking at yourself while you really look for spies. If you have mirrored sunglasses, you can use them as well. Take them off and pretend to clean them while checking out the reflection in the lenses.

You can also use something called **cover for action**. This is when you do something like stop to tie your shoe

SPY TIP:

Following someone is called shadowing them, and the person doing the following is sometimes called a shadow. You've got to keep an eye out for these shadows, but it's important that you keep an eye out for the normal kind of shadow as well!

Shadows can be a dead giveaway that someone's following you, but they can also get you caught if you're the one doing the following so keep an eye on where the sun is casting your shadow!

Casing the Joint

It's also always important to know the areas that you go to all the time. Sometimes, you should just walk by to make sure everything is like you remember it. This is called **casing**.

It's always a good idea to carefully case out an area you might want to use for operations. That way you know if things move around a lot. It might even be a good idea to take some pictures. Then you can compare the area to the photos a few days later to make sure nothing has changed. Then, even if you're being followed by other spies, you'll have the home court advantage and be able to use that to escape them.

Casing also helps you to figure out the right time and place to do your spying. Is there a time when the area's more crowded? Do you see the same people over and over again? Are there hiding places available if you need one?

SPY TIP:

Try the ABC Surveillance exercise again. This time, take turns being the Rabbit and see who can lose the surveillance team the fastest. You can even have the Rabbit hide something. Which of you is good enough at avoiding surveillance and hide your object without anyone seeing you do it?

Quit Bugging Me!

Bug is a term for any device that lets you listen in on another area without being seen. Baby monitors, which let moms hear what's happening in their baby's room at all times, work like a bug. A hidden tape recorder is a kind of bug, too. Professional spies have tiny, almost invisible bugs that they can plant on almost anything without being seen: on jackets and hats, in books, telephones, lamps, or even vases of flowers.

Look around your HQ. Where could a spy plant bugs? Remember to look for bugs (or anyone who might be listening in) before you have a meeting with your fellow spies, no matter where you are—in your HQ, your bedroom, or even out at the pizza place.

On the TV show *Veronica Mars*, Veronica plants a bug in her guidance counselor's stapler, so that she can listen to the guidance counselor interview all of the suspects.

Bug Extermination

Here's a great exercise to practice your bug-detection skills. (It will also help you notice if anyone ever messes with you HQ.)

First, you should gather together a group of co-spies. Take some caps off of old milk jugs or juice containers and wrap them in tin foil. These are going to be your bugs. Now, have one person wait outside while the others hide the bugs around the room. Then, let the person outside back in and have him try to find all the bugs. Then switch, so everyone gets a chance. Did you find all the bugs? Keep practicing. No one will be able to bug you again!

Real Spy Gadgets

This shoe has a radio transmitter hidden in it! The transmitter was made by the KGB during the Cold War to help them listen in on secret conversations. They would place the transmitter, microphone, and batteries into their target's shoe. Once the target was wearing the shoes and the transmitter was activated, the target's conversations were transmitted to a nearby spy post.

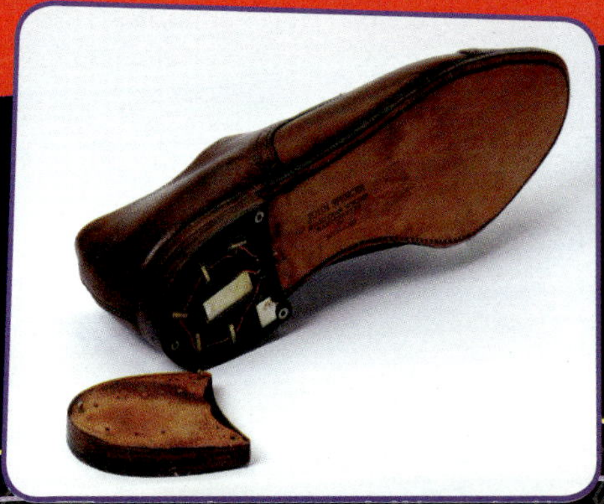

Mission ACCOMPLISHED!

Congrats! You've successfully mastered techniques for following, watching, and making sure you're not being watched. You know the ABCs of following, how to shoot from the hip, and how to avoid being bugged. Your enemies will never see you coming. You're going to be a terrific spy!

RED CORDELLO

Writer

Red Cordello and his sister Violet own and run a detective agency on the Lower East Side of Manhattan. When not working, Red enjoys reading Victorian mystery novels, installing secret passages in his apartment, and playing with his cat, Indigo.

TONY AND JONNA MENDEZ

Consultants

Tony and Jonna spent their careers at the CIA. They worked overseas protecting American spies and the foreign assets working for the U.S. government. They were specialists in disguise and documents. Tony Mendez was named as one of the CIA's top spies in the last 50 years.

Glossary

These are the spy terms you need to know for continued undercover success!

ABC Surveillance – Basic foot surveillance using three people to follow a Rabbit

Bug – A small listening device that can be hidden almost anywhere

Case – To inspect and study an area for future operations

Countersurveillence – The practice of avoiding surveillance

Cover for Action – The story a spy invents to explain his actions

Misinformation – False information given to throw off the enemy

Mobile Surveillance – Surveillance carried out on a moving target

Mole – A spy who works for one country but is secretly spying for another country

Rabbit – The target of ABC surveillance

Shooting from the Hip – Holding the camera at hip level and taking pictures without looking

Static Surveillance – Surveillance of a specific area carried out from one place

Surveillance – Closely watching another person's movements and activities

Surveillance Detection Run – A technique to check and see if you are being followed or observed

Surveillance Post – A long-term place from which to conduct surveillance

Target – A person or place that is the subject of an intelligence operation